Alphabets & Ornaments

Memories of a Lifetime

Anna Corba

Sterling Publishing Co., Inc. New York
A Sterling/Chapelle Book

Art Designer: Anna Corba

If you have any questions or comments, please contact:
Chapelle, Ltd., Inc., P.O. Box 9252, Ogden, UT 84409
(801) 621-2777 • (801) 621-2788 Fax
e-mail: chapelle@chapelleltd.com
Web site: www.chapelleltd.com

The designs and illustrations in this book may be used for graphic, craft, and
publication applications without special permission and free of charge.
Commercial use of artwork contained in this volume is forbidden under law
without the written permission of the publisher.

10 9 8 7 6 5 4 3 2

Published by Sterling Publishing Co., Inc.
387 Park Avenue South, New York, NY 10016
© 2005 by Sterling Publishing Co., Inc.
Distributed in Canada by Sterling Publishing
c/o Canadian Manda Group, 165 Dufferin Street
Toronto, Ontario, Canada M6K 3H6
Distributed in Great Britain by Chrysalis Books Group PLC,
The Chrysalis Building, Bramley Road, London W10 6SP, England
Distributed in Australia by Capricorn Link (Australia) Pty. Ltd.
P. O. Box 704, Windsor, NSW 2756, Australia
Printed and Bound in China
All Rights Reserved

Sterling ISBN 1-4027-1995-7

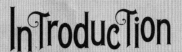

InTroducTion

I magine having hundreds of rare, vintage images right at your fingertips. With our *Memories of a Lifetime* series, that's exactly what you get. We've scoured antique stores, estate sales, and other outlets to find one-of-a-kind images to give your projects the flair that only old-time artwork can provide. From Victorian postcards to hand-painted beautiful borders and frames, it would take years to acquire a collection like this. However, with this easy-to-use resource, you'll have them all—right here, right now.

Each image has been reproduced to the highest quality standard for photocopying and scanning; reduce or enlarge them to suit your needs. A CD-Rom containing all of the images in digital form is included, enabling you to use them for any computer project over and again. If you prefer to use them as they're printed, simply cut them out—they're printed on one side only.

Perfect for paper crafting, scrapbooking, and fabric transfers, *Memories of a Lifetime* books will inspire you to explore new avenues of creativity. We've included a sampling of ideas to get you started, but the best part is using your imagination to create your own fabulous projects. Be sure to look for other books in this series as we continue to search the markets for wonderful vintage images.

How to Use this Book

General Instructions:

These images are printed on one side only, making it easy to simply cut out the desired image. However, you'll probably want to use them again, so we have included a CD-Rom which contains all of the images individually as well as in the page layout form. The CDs can be used with both PC and Mac formats. Just pop in the disk. On a PC, the file will immediately open to the Home page, which will walk you through how to view and print the images. For Macintosh® users, you will simply double-click on the icon to open. The images may also be incorporated into your computer projects using simple imaging software that you can purchase specifically for this purpose—a perfect choice for digital scrapbooking. The reference numbers printed on the back of each image in the book are the same ones used on the CD, which will allow you to easily find the image you are looking for. The numbering consists of the book abbreviation, the page number, the image number, and the file format. The first file number (located next to the page number) is for the entire page. For example, AO01-001.jpg would be the entire image for page 1 of *Alphabets & Ornaments*. The second file number is for the top-right image. The numbers continue in a counterclockwise fashion.

Once you have resized your images, added text, created a scrapbook page, etc., you are ready to print them out. Printing on cream or white cardstock, particularly a textured variety, creates a more authentic look. You won't be able to tell that it's a reproduction! If you don't have access to a computer or printer, that's ok. Most photocopy centers can resize and print your images for a nominal fee, or they have do-it-yourself machines that are easy to use.

Ideas for using the images:

Scrapbooking: These images are perfect for both heritage and modern scrapbook pages. Simply use the image as a frame, accent piece, or border. For those of you with limited time, or limited design ability, the page layouts in this book have been created so that you can use them as they are. Simply print out or photocopy the desired page, attach a photograph into one of the boxes, and you have a beautiful scrapbook page in minutes. For a little dimension, add a ribbon or charm. Be sure to print your images onto acid-free cardstock so the pages will last a lifetime.

Cards: Some computer programs allow images to be inserted into a card template, simplifying cardmaking. If this is not an option, simply use the images as accent pieces on the front or inside of the card. Use a bone folder to score the card's fold to create a more professional look.

Decoupage/Collage Projects: For decoupage or collage projects, photocopy or print the image onto a thinner paper such as copier paper. Thin paper adheres to projects more effectively. Decoupage medium glues and seals the project, creating a gloss or matte finish when dry, thus protecting the image. Vintage images are beautiful when decoupaged to cigar boxes, glass plates, and even wooden plaques. The possibilities are endless.

Fabric Arts: Vintage images can be used in just about any fabric craft imaginable: wall hangings, quilts, bags, or baby bibs. Either transfer the image onto the fabric by using a special iron-on paper, or by printing the image directly onto the fabric, using a temporary iron-on stabilizer that stabilizes the fabric to feed through a printer. These items are available at most craft and sewing stores. If the item will be washed, it is better to print directly on the fabric. For either method, follow the instructions on the package.

Wood Transfers: It is now possible to "print" images on wood. Use this exciting technique to create vintage plaques, clocks, frames, and more. A simple, inexpensive transfer tool is available at most large craft or home improvement stores, or online from various manufacturers. You simply place the photocopy of the image you want, face down, onto the surface and use the tool to transfer the image onto the wood. This process requires a copy from a laser printer, which means you will probably have to get your copies made at a copy center. Refer to manufacturer's instructions for additional details. There are other transfer products available that can be used with wood. Choose the one that is easiest for you.

Gallery of ideas

These *Alphabet & Ornament* images can be used in a variety of projects: cards, scrapbook pages, and decoupage projects to name a few. The images can be used as they are shown in the layout, or you can copy and clip out individual images, or even portions or multitudes of images. The following pages contain a collection of ideas to inspire you to use your imagination and create one-of-a-kind treasures. Vintage alphabets do not always include all of the letters as we now know them, and sometimes only a few of the letters are available. Hopefully, we have given you enough of a variety that you will find something to suit your needs.

Scrapbook pages don't always have to include photographs. This page uses various food-related images joined together into a fun collage. A snippet of vintage ledger paper creates a nice background for journaling. Use old-fashioned photo corners to tuck some of your elements into place. Rubber-stamped images complete the page.

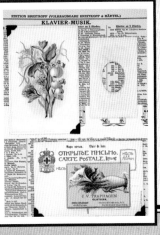

This project shows how simple it is to add a photograph to a postcard image. The photo at left shows the images as they appear in the book. The finished scrapbook page below demonstrates how you can utilize the images for a quick and easy scrapbook page.

Family Scrapbook Page

Use deckle-edged scissors to cut out your photographs and images. This adds to the vintage feel of the page. Don't feel like you have to use an entire background page—use pieces and strips of newsprint and sheet music for more variety.

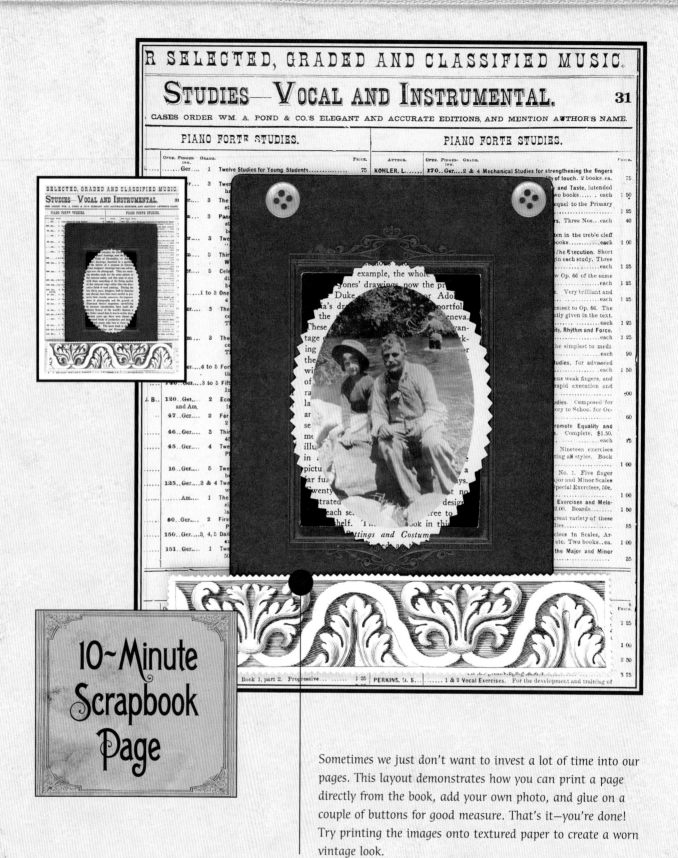

10~Minute Scrapbook Page

Sometimes we just don't want to invest a lot of time into our pages. This layout demonstrates how you can print a page directly from the book, add your own photo, and glue on a couple of buttons for good measure. That's it—you're done! Try printing the images onto textured paper to create a worn vintage look.

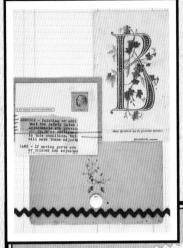

This project is another example of a simple alteration of an existing page in the book. The page was printed a little bit smaller than a normal scrapbook page and trimmed with scallop-edged scissors. It was then angled and adhered to another background page.

B is for Baby Page

Use images in this book to create your own unique cards and invitations. This vintage child post-card was perfect for the front of a baby shower invitation, which was then used on the scrap-book page documenting the event.

January 6
Betsy's baby shower ... what a wonderful day

N°. 4.

Alphabet Canisters

Decorated canisters make great packaging for gifts. This particular set would be perfect for a new arrival, filled with baby toiletries, T-shirts, or bibs.

Make these charming canisters by wrapping copies of sheet music, or other background paper, around the canisters and securing with double-stick tape. Copy and trim alphabet letters and trading card images and adhere to the canisters with a glue stick. Use assorted ribbons and trims to embellish.

Bonjour Memory Box

Choose a decorative frame that works well behind your desired image. Copy and trim the images and adhere to the box top. For an authentic touch, add a postmark, using a rubber stamp. Decorate the box with pom-pom trim.

It is easy to make a great memory box like this. Simply use a purchased wooden or papier-mâché box. Paint the bottom of the box with cream acrylic paint and the top with sage green.

Tack striped ribbon trim along top and bottom of frame with craft glue. A wooden bingo piece and vintage velvet leaves add the perfect finishing touch.

Vintage Photo Display

This is a fabulous way to display old photographs. Copy the desired images from the book and make a background collage. Make certain your collage includes a frame.

Decoupage the collage to a ⅛" piece of fiberboard, using a matte medium. Paint the back and edges of the board black. Paste the photo into the center of the frame.

Cover your desired scrapbook with background
paper. Choose an image that relates to the
book's content. Adhere to the cover with a
glue stick. Tuck a piece of ribbon trim into
photo corners and attach a velvet leaf sprig.
Tie silk ribbon through the binding and leave
a generous bow.

Precious Scrapbook Cover

Decorative Tray

Paint a wooden tray deep red on the inside and black around the edges and bottom. Copy an alphabet from the book, trim with decorative scissors, and decoupage to the tray with matte medium. Trim your desired postcard image with decorative scissors and glue to the center. Add ornamental bird and flower images. Postmark with a rubber stamp. Finish the tray with an acrylic varnish.

AO01-002

AO01-003

AO01-004

AO01-005

AO01-007

AO01-006

1 — AO01-001

AO02-002

AO02-003

AO02-006

AO02-004

AO02-005

AO02-001

2

SOUVENIR POST CARD

Whistle
Whip
Wolf

2.50 POLSKA

450.

Roma Derna Ancona

APPLICAZIONI

Como Genova Urbino

AO03-002

AO03-003

AO03-001

AO04-002

AO04-007

AO04-003

AO04-006

AO04-005

AO04-004

AO04-001 4

Sept 22 | chk #
34 3

Pac. Tel. Co   2 mos.
S. V. Water   3 "
Linehan & Co.   hauling
Guy T. Wayman
  Appraising land values
     for estate purposes

William A. Magee —
  Appraising land values
     for estate purposes.

Carl Anderson —
Town & Country Club —
J. D. West   harness repairs
La Grande
Dr. Quinlan   vet.
Hoffmann & Sons
C. A. Bowman
Pac. Tel. Co.
G.

20 HELVETIA

20 HELVETIA

les draft

lc

lc dr.

CHEER UP

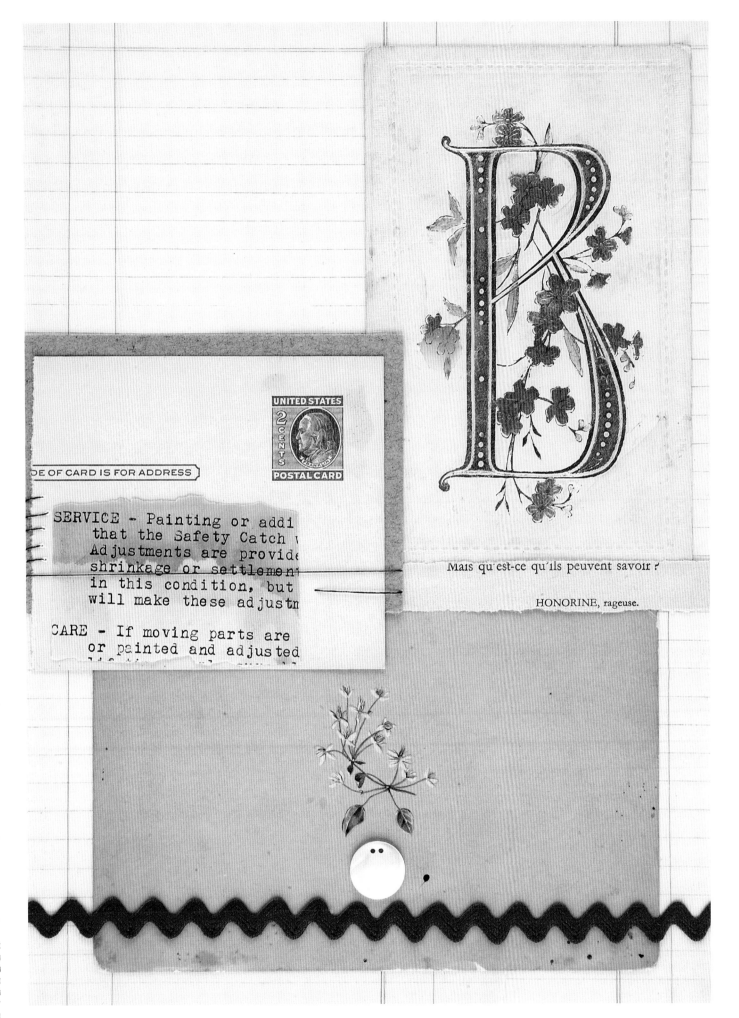

DE OF CARD IS FOR ADDRESS

UNITED STATES
2 CENTS
B.FRANKLIN
POSTAL CARD

SERVICE - Painting or addi
that the Safety Catch v
Adjustments are provide
shrinkage or settlemen
in this condition, but
will make these adjustn

CARE - If moving parts are
or painted and adjusted

Mais qu'est-ce qu'ils peuvent savoir ?

HONORINE, rageuse.

AO05-002

AO05-005

AO05-004

AO05-003

5 AO05-001

AO06-002

AO06-003

AO06-004   AO06-007

                                                      AO06-006

          AO06-005

Summary - 1919

Jan.
Jan.
Feb.
Mar.
Apr.
May
June
July
Aug.
Nov.
Dec.

18
337
165
20
72
195
336
285   86
2277
5009
3047
1735
1631
104

Cyclamen
DIFFIDENCE

Flowers are lovely;
Love is flower-like
Friendship is
A sheltering tree.

362   "   " Palos Verdes
363   "   " Brway-Pac Ave-
364 Santa Barbara - Naples
369 Wardell

ART INSTITUTE OF CHICAGO
PERMANENT COLLECTIONS OF WORKS OF ART
CURRENT EXHIBITIONS ∴ SCHOOL OF THE ART
INSTITUTE ∴ RYERSON LIBRARY (OF BOOKS
ON ART) ∴ ART INSTITUTE LECTURE SERIES
ART INSTITUTE EXTENSION

THE SOWER
By ALBIN POLASEK, American, 1879—
Heroic Bronze Figure
Friends of American Art, 1916

POST CARD   Carte Postale   POSTKARTE
BRIEFKAART — POSTKAART
CARTOLINA POSTALE — ОТКРЫТОЕ ПИСЬМО — TARJETA POSTAL

Reward of Merit
Presented to

By

Teacher.

AO07-002

AO07-003

AO07-004

AO07-005

AO08-002

AO08-003

CZERNY

Selected Pianoforte Studies

Arranged in systematic order &c.,

BY

Ed. Domenico Trampetti - Napoli

NEW YORK
Edward Schuberth & Co.,
(J.F.H.MEYER.)
11 EAST 22ND ST

To my
Valentine.

Publisher Walter Wirths, New York, City. 318 D.   Germany

AO09-002

AO09-003   AO09-008

AO09-004

AO09-007

AO09-005

AO09-006

9 — AO09-001

AO10-001

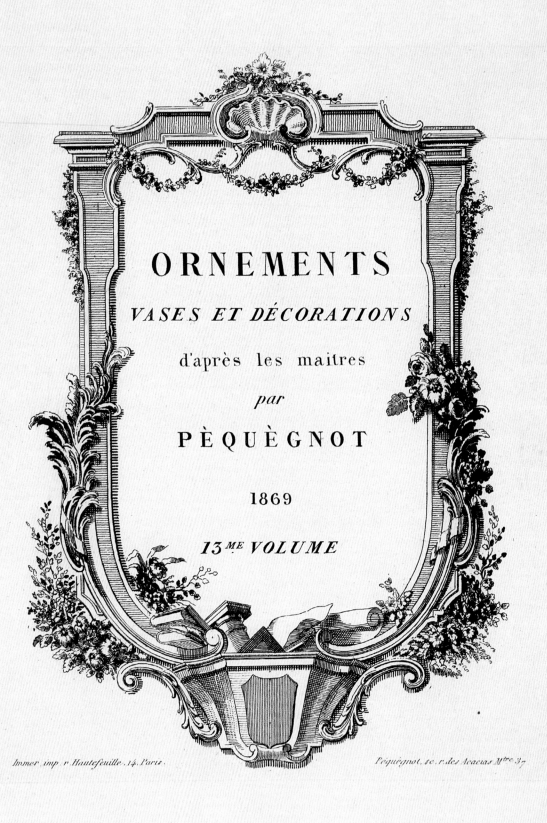

ORNEMENTS

VASES ET DÉCORATIONS

d'après les maitres

par

PÈQUÈGNOT

1869

13ᴹᴱ VOLUME

Immer. imp. r. Hautefeuille. 14. Paris.   Pèquègnot, sc. r. des Acacias Mᵗʳᵉ 37

To Auntie.

In the golden chain
of friend-ship regard me
as a link.
Your niece
Lena Pearson

Dear Sister
A Smooth Sea
never made a
skillful marina

your loving
Sister
Libbie Pearson

AO11-002

AO11-003

AO12-002

AO12-003

AO12-007

AO12-004

AO12-006

AO12-005

AO12-001   12

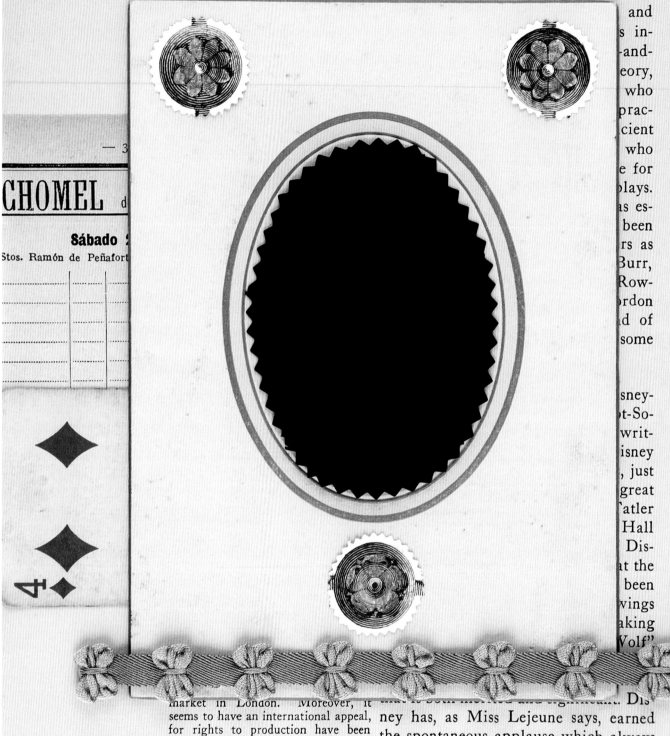

CHOMEL

Sábado 2

Stos. Ramón de Peñafort

— 3

4♦

and
s in-
-and-
eory,
who
prac-
cient
who
e for
olays.
as es-
been
rs as
Burr,
Row-
rdon
d of
some

sney-
t-So-
writ-
isney
, just
great
atler
Hall
Dis-
t the
been
vings
aking
Volf"

market in London. Moreover, it
seems to have an international appeal,
for rights to production have been
sold to thirty foreign countries, in-
cluding the West Indies and Turkey.

ney has, as Miss Lejeune says, earned
the spontaneous applause which always
greets the appearance of one of his lov-

Dis

THE LINNET
If, I were a Linnet
I'd build my nest
With "MILE END" Cotton,
Smoothest and best.

...ing room on the Seattle stage. The

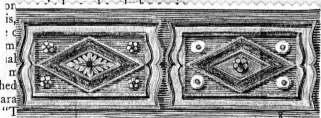

...ing of genius being the capac...
...king pains when she hailed Dis-
...the greatest talkie producer.
There are rumors, on the one
hand, that Mickey Mouse is to be aban-

tators, who patiently had sat two
hours to see Miss Cornell, gave her
a rousing welcome when the curtain

AO13-002

AO13-003   AO13-006

AO13-004

AO13-005

AO13-001

AO14-002

AO14-003

AO14-004   AO14-006

AO14-005

AO14-001 14

FOR TAXES 1885.

No. 1151

TREASURER'S OFFICE, FURNAS COUNTY, NEB.

Beaver City, *May 4"* 1886

RECEIVED of *H. B. Fordmer*

Four and _____ 54 DOLLARS,
                              100

in full for the following Taxes for the year 1885.

Co Bond 6

DESCRIPTION	Sec. or Lot	Twp or Blk	Rng	Acres	Value	Labor Tax	AMOUNT	Int.	TOTAL
					$		$ Cts.		
E ½ DE ¼	19	4	21	80	155				4 54

Sch'l Dist.
Bond Levi's

Mills
No. 4, 2
No. 6, 3
No. 10, 3
No. 15, 10
No. 18, 3
No. 19, 3
No. 21, 2
No. 24, 2

Receipt

QCR. 1885.

HONI SOIT QUI MAL Y PENSE

Reward of Merit.

Presented to

_____

Teacher.

Duplicates or Enlargements can be

furnished from this Negative.

No. 287

County Treasurer's Office, Furnas County, Nebraska.

Beaver City, Neb., Aug 8

Received of H. B. Gardner

in full of the Taxes for the year 1880:

DESCRIPTION	Sec. or Lot	Town or Blk.	Rng.	Acres	Amount Tax	Advertising	Interest
	9	4	21	80	459		12

State General 2 Mills
State Sink 3/8
State School 3 1/4
University 2 Mills
County General 2 11.3
Road
Bridge 13
Dist. School 4 1/2

A. E. Harry, Treasurer.

(ORIGINAL.)

$4 71

STATE JOURNAL CO., Printers, Lincoln, Neb.

AO15-002   AO15-006

AO15-003   AO15-005

AO15-004

AO15-001

AO16-001

Great A
Bouncing B.

a b c
d e f g h
i j k l m

n o p q r
s t u v w
x y z

AO17-002

AO17-003

AO18-002

AO18-006

AO18-005

AO18-003

AO18-004

AO18-001 18

41

AO19-002

AO19-003

AO19-004

AO19-005

AO19-006

AO19-001

AO20-002

AO20-003   AO20-006

                                                AO20-005

AO20-004

Favorite Songs by Pearl G. Curran

RAIN

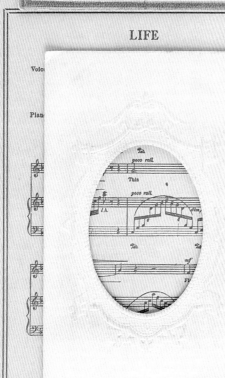

LIFE

HO! MR. PIPER

New York · G. SCHIRMER · Boston

A 624

KLAVIER-MUSIK.

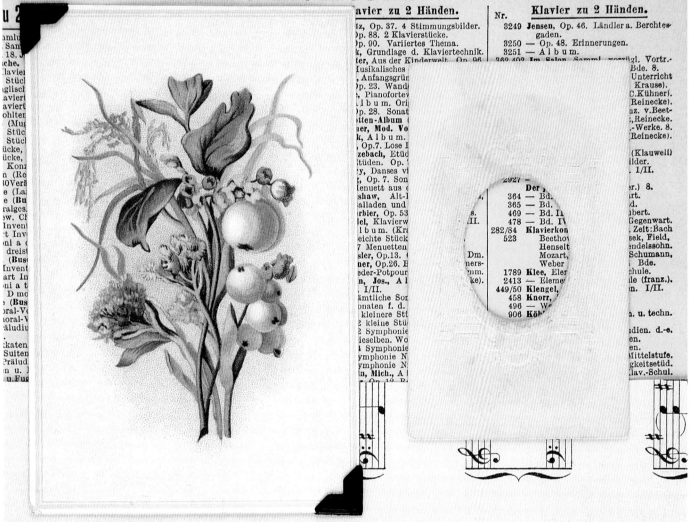

AO21-002

AO21-003   AO21-007

AO21-004

AO21-005

AO21-006

AO21-001

AO22-001

Le Déjeuner

5

Darne de Flétan Antoinette

Les Calories 170   Les Carbohydrates 5.6 gr.

Purée d'Epinards et de Champignons

Les Calories 60   Les Carbohydrates 1.4 gr.

Poire et Fromage

Les Calories 155   Les Carbohydrates 25.2 gr

Total
Calories
385

Total
Carbohydrates
32.2 gr.

A HAPPY NEW YEAR TO YOU

CARTE POSTALE

La Correspondance de ce côté n'est pas acceptée par tous les pays (Se renseigner à la poste)

CORRESPONDANCE

ADRESSE

M

AO23-002

AO23-003   AO23-005

AO23-004

AO23-001

AO24-002

AO24-009

AO24-003

AO24-008

AO24-004

AO24-005

AO24-007

AO24-006

AO24-001 24

Rensselaerville Sept 2 1851

Dear Brother

that ... to go home

with him as he was going directly to R ville if

Publisher Walter Wirths, New York, City. 319 O.   Germany

Publisher Walter Wirths, New York, City. 319 N.   Germany

NOVELTY
BEAUTY & FASHION
MAISON DEMOREST.
AGENCIES EVERYWHERE
RELIABLE PATTERNS
IN SIZES
ILLUSTRATED & DESCRIBED

HE LOVES ME

WELCOME

HAPPY MORNING.

A a b c d e f g h i l m n o p q r s t v u x y z.

a b c d e f g h i l m n o p q r s t v u x y z

good wishes for you.

POLSKA

AO25-002

AO25-003

AO25-007

AO25-004

AO25-005

AO25-006

25 AO25-001

AO26-002

AO26-005

AO26-003

AO26-004

AO26-001   26

P
Q
R
S
T
U
V
W
X
Y
Z

piece

G

This is a whole pie.

This is a

| piece. |
| part. |

(pieces)

pierce

pierce

pierce

Bob | pierced / punched | a hole in the paper.

(pierces   pierced   piercing)

elephant
el-e-phant
elephant
elephant

HIS TUSKS WERE CLEANED WITH IVORINE

IVORINE IS A BIG THING

pigeon

Ii

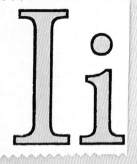

This bird is a | pigeon. / dove. |

Some people have pet pigeons.

(pigeons)

This is a <u>family</u>.

In this <u>family</u> there is the father, mother and two children.

(families)

family
fam-i-ly
family
family

This is

It helps

Do you

Through the NEW YEAR may happiness ATTEND YOU.

Mary ca

as <u>far</u>

Grandm

The

in

The

th

ckets.

(fares)

faraway
far-a-way
faraway
faraway

fare
fare
fare

F
G
H
I
J
K
L
M
N
O
P
Q
R
S
T
U
V
W
X
Y
Z

AO27-002

AO27-003

AO27-004

AO27-005

27 AO27-001

AO28-002

AO28-004

AO28-003

D for our Doggie
  With cap on his head.

F for the Fruit

U is an Umbrella
To keep off the snow.

W is a Wag[on]
[l]raden

[ar]e the Visitors
[and] friends we know.

20

AO29-003

AO30-002

AO30-003

AO30-004   AO30-005

A GIFT of LOVE.

AO31-002

AO31-003   AO31-005

AO31-004

AO31-001

AO32-002

AO32-003

AO32-004

AO32-005

CASES ORDER WM. A. POND & CO.'S ELEGANT AND ACCURATE EDITIONS, AND MENTION AUTHOR'S NAME.

PIANO FORTE STUDIES.

OPUS.	FINGER-ING.	GRADE.		PRICE.
......Ger...		1	Twelve Studies for Young Students..............	75
100..Ger...		3	Twe...	
81..Ger...		3	The...	
......Am...		3	Pan...	
F... 20..Ger...		3	Twe...	
B... ......Am...		5	Thir...	
B... ......Ger...		5	Cele...	
......139.......1 to 3			One...	
......299..Ger...		3	The...	
......299..Am...		3	The...	
......337..Ger...4 to 5			For...	
......740..Ger...3 to 5			Fift...	
J. B... 120..Ger... and Am		2	Eco...	
......47..Ger...		2	For...	
......46..Ger...		3	Thir...	
......45..Ger...		4	Twe...	
......16..Ger...		5	Twe...	
......125..Ger...3 & 4			Twe...	
......Am...		1	The...	
......50..Ger...		2	First...	
......156..Ger...3, 4, 5			Dail...	
......151..Ger...		1	Twe... 50	

PIANO FORTE STUDIES.

AUTHOR.	OPUS. FINGER-ING.	GRADE.		PRICE.
KOHLER, L......	170..Ger...	2 & 4	Mechanical Studies for strengthening the fingers ...lity of touch. 2 books. ea.	75
			...and Taste, intended ...wo books..... . each	1 50
			...equel to the Primary	1 25
			...rs. Three Nos..each	40
			...ten in the treble cleff ...books......... each	1 00
			...The Execution. Short ...in each study. Three ....each	1 25
			...w Op. 66 of the same ....each	1 25
			...s. Very brilliant and ....each	1 25
			...ement to Op. 66. The ...lly given in the text. ....each	1 25
			...ity, Rhythm and Force. ....each	1 25
			...he simplest to medi- ....each	90
			...tudies, for advanced ....each	1 50
			...ens weak fingers, and ...rapid execution and	40
			...dies. Composed for ...ory to School for Oc-	60
			...romote Equality and ...s. Complete, $1.50. ....each	75
			...Nineteen exercises ...ting all styles. Book	1 00
			...No. 1. Five finger ...ajor and Minor Scales ...pecial Exercises, 50c.	1 00
			...Exercises and Melo- ...2.00. Boards.......	1 50
			...great variety of these ...ies...............	80
			...cises in Scales, Ar- ...etc. Two books..ea.	1 00
			...the Major and Minor	80

example, the whole
...jones' drawings, now the pr...
...Duke of Devonshire, or Adol...
...a's drawings, deposited in a portfol...
...the shelves of a museum in Geneva.
These designers' drawings have one advantage over the photograph. They are working sketches made for the scene painter or the costume maker, and they seem to carry with them something of the living quality of the rehearsal stage rather than the decorative finish of easel painting. During the last thirty years, designers, both in America and abroad, have been more careful to preserve their records; moreover, the improvement in photography and the growth of illustrated theatre magazines, specializing in accurate reproduction, have made the picture history of the world's theatres a far fuller record than it was in earlier days. Twenty years ago there were almost no ...trated books of production and desig... each season adds two or three to ...shelf. The latest book in thi... *...ttings and Costum...* ...ed at t...

					PRICE.
					15
R...					1 00
A...					25
					3 75
2.	1	Fifty Lessons. Book 1, part 2. Progressive.........	1 25	PERKINS, W. S...	......1 & 2 Vocal Exercises. For the development and training of
		Book 1, complete....................	2 50		the voice. Two books. No. 1, 60. No. 2...... 1 00
9.	2	Fifty Lessons. Book 2, part 1. Melodious and easy...	1 25	SALMSON, F...	......2 Practical Exercises. To develop the compass and flexi- ...bility of the voice, and form an expressive style.

ABCDEFGHI
JKLMNOPQR
STUVWXYZ&

OUVERTÜRE

FÜR PIANOFORTE
ZU ZWEI HÄNDEN

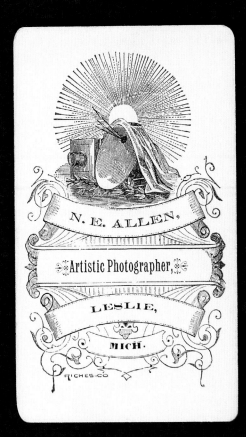

AO33-002

AO33-003

AO33-008

AO33-007

AO33-005

AO33-004

AO33-006

33 AO33-001

AO34-002

AO34-003

Frames.—

…nt 1760.

MDarly sculp.

Ercolano Sondrio Livorn

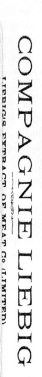

COMPAGNIE LIEBIG

LIEBIG'S EXTRACT OF MEAT Co (LIMITED)

Sample of SEELY'S PERFUME.
Compliments of
McCULLOUGH, REQUA & TUTTON,
DRUGGISTS.
Sioux Falls, Dakota.

AO35-002

AO35-003

AO35-006

AO35-005

AO35-004

AO35-001

AO36-001

A "MAID OF ATHENS!"

3/4 7 mm 2/3

3/4 7 mm 2/3

Alberti Buonarroti Canova Paddi Este

Fiesole Giotto Lipp Imola Renn Riberi

Morelli Pardi Arcagna Palladio Quadri

Raffaello Sansovino Tintoretto Albertini

Vasari Wigan Ximenes York Zosimo

1 2 3 4 5 6 7 8 9 0

Gio. Tonso Modelli di Calligrafia

Litografica DOYEN - MARCHI TORINO

AO37-001

AO38-002

AO38-003

AO38-005

AO38-004

AO38-001 — 38

S equéntia sancti Euangélij secúndùm Lucam.

IN illo témpore: Postquam consummáti sunt dies octo, vt circumciderétur puer: vocátum est nomen eius Iesus, quod vocátum est ab Angelo priúsquam in útero conciperétur. Credo.

Offertorium. Tui sunt cæli, & tua est terra: orbem terrárum, & plenitúdinem eius tu fundásti: iustítia & iudícium præparátio sedis tuæ.

Secreta.

in tuis iustificatiónibus. Psalm. Beáti immaculáti in via: qui ámbulant in lege Dómini. ℣. Glória Patri.

Oratio.

...tiorum mala mortífica; vt fidem tuam, quam lingua nostra lóquitur, étiam móribus vita fateâtur. Per Dóminum nostrum.

ctauis in Dominica venerit, dici-

Fair
Hopes

Clouds of snowy blossom,
     Flushed with tints of rose;
Sheaths of brown, which opening
     Tender leaves disclose;
Buds of fairy beauty,
     Grouped in perfect sprays
These are coming for us
     With the sweet spring days!

IN OCTAV

S. Stephani Protomartyris.
Introitus.

Psal.
118.

Ederunt príncipes, & aduérsum me loque-bántur: & iníqui per-secúti sunt me: ádiu-ua me, Dómine Deus meus, quia seruus tuus exercebâtur populo. Surrexérunt autem qui-dam de synagóga, quæ appellâtur Libertinôrum, & Cyrenénsium, & Alexandrinôrum, & eôrum, qui erant à Cilícia, & Asia, disputántes cum Stéphano: & non póterant resístere sapiéntiæ, & Spirítui, qui loquebâtur. Audiéntes autem

Cap.
7.8

D 3

AO39-006   AO39-005   AO39-004   AO39-003   AO39-002

AO39-008   AO39-007

AO39-015   AO39-010   AO39-009

AO39-012   AO39-011

AO39-014   AO39-013

AO39-016

AO39-017

AO39-001

AO40-002

AO40-003

AO40-004

AO40-007

AO40-005

AO40-006

AO40-001 40

EJERCICIO N.º 0 (3) (1)

FRASES U ORACIONES PRECEDI-
DAS DE SIGNOS QUE LAS RE-
PRESENTAN EN EL ANÁLISIS
QUE SIGUE......

A) Nuestros vecinos duermen
B) Este vejestorio se lava
C) Cuentas muchas cosas de América
Ch) Todos quieren trabajar en el vehículo
D) Los muchachos corrían por las calles
E) Los ladrones robaron un vestido

F) La naturale
G) El tribunal
H) Eligieron p
I) Estas niñas
J) Así mata
K) Eusebio es

DESCOMPOSICIÓN DE DICHAS

SIGNOS	ANALÓGICO							
				CLASIFICACIÓN DE				
	VARIABLES			INVARIABLES			E	
	POR LAS IDEAS QUE REPRESENTAN O POR EL OFICIO QUE DESP...						SUS S	
	Substantivos							
	1			E. M.	Preposi-
ciones		Determinante del	Monosílabos
					7			
A)	vecinos							
B)	vejestorio							
C)	cosas, Amér							
CH)	vehículo							
D)	muchachos, c							
E)	ladrones, ves							
F)	naturaleza, pa							
G)	tribunal, tes							
H)	presidente, di							

5064. PARIS
La Grande Roue

RÉPUBLIQUE FRANÇAISE 15c

THE PINK. THE PEAR.

SOUVENIR POST CARD

P

ARTHUR P. SCHMIDT'S
OCTAVO EDITION.

GIO. TONSO MODELLI DI CALLIGRAFIA

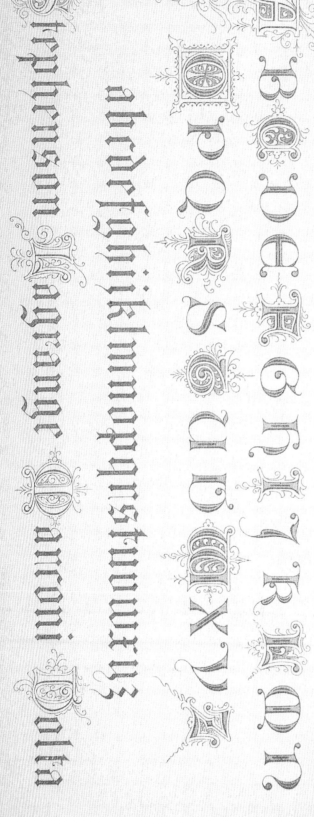

Stephenson Lagrange Marconi Volta

abcdefghijklmnopqrstuvwxyz

ABCDEFGHIJKLMNOPQRSTUVWXYZ

LITOGRAFICA
DOYEN - MARCHISIO
TORINO

Otto Pettersson's
FOTOGRAFISKA
ATELIER
LUND.

Originalplåten bevaras för framtida
efterbeställningar.

SIR HENRY WOTTON

So, when my mistress shall be seen
   In form and beauty of her mind,
By virtue first, then choice, a Queen,
   Tell me, if she were not design'd
   Th' eclipse and glory of her kind.

BEN JONSON.

TO CELIA.

DRINK to me only with thine eyes,
   And I will pledge with mine;
Or leave a kiss but in the cup;
   And I'll not look for wine.
The thirst that from the soul doth rise
   Doth ask a drink divine;
But might I of Jove's nectar sup,
   I would not change for thine.

I sent thee late a rosy wreath,
   Not so much honouring thee
As giving it a hope that there
   It could not wither'd be;
But thou thereon didst only breathe,
   And sent'st it back to me;
Since when it grows, and smells, I swear,
   Not of itself but thee!

AO41-002

AO41-003

AO41-004

AO41-005

AO41-006

AO41-001

AO42-002

AO42-003

AO42-004

AO42-008

AO42-007

AO42-005

AO42-006

AO42-001 42

Winter 105

Copyrighted by Frank Vernon, N.Y. 1882

True love watches over thee

FIRST EXERCISE (TOP TO BOTTOM)

to lowercase letters

LES CINQ SENS

PER SOLEM PINGO

V. MANDERS
The Studio
HOE STREET
WALTHAMSTOW
COPIES CAN ALWAYS BE HAD

MARION & CO.
REGISTERED

London.

Raphael Tuck & Sons Collo-Photo Series. No. 1564.
ART PUBLISHERS TO THEIR MAJESTIES THE KING & QUEEN.

By Appointment

TUCK'S POST CARD

CARTE POSTALE

FOR ADDRESS ONLY

Compliments of
M. S. JONES & CO.,
Dealers in all kinds of
FURNITURE.
Undertaking a Specialty.
LOWVILLE, N. Y.

AO43-002

AO43-008

AO43-003

AO43-007

AO43-005

AO43-004

AO43-006

43 — AO43-001

AO44-002

AO44-003

AO44-004

AO44-005

ABCDEFGHIJKLMNOP
QRSTUVWXYZ&

abcdefghijklmnopqrstuvwxyz
.,:;!?'""-Thffffffiffl1234567890$

SIROP DE
Citron

PUR SUCRE

DOUIN & J.

❖TEEPLE'S❖

FRENCH LIGHT

❖GALLERIES❖

USES THE

INSTANTANEOUS

DRY PLATE PROCESS

WOOSTER & ASHLAND, O.

SAVON

A L'EXTRAIT DE SON

PARFUMERIE

DEROUBAIX & Cie

4, Rue des Manneliers – LILLE

DEROUBAIX & Cie
PARFUMEURS — LILLE
MARQUE DÉPOSÉE

AO45-007

AO45-002

AO45-006

AO45-003

AO45-005

AO45-004

AO45-001

AO46-002

AO46-003

BLUE OCTAVO SERIES
SECULAR

HAROLD FLAMMER
INCORPORATED
PUBLISHER
NEW YORK

A CHOICE SELECTION OF
TWO-PART CHORUSES

For Treble Voices

No.	Price
7001	.15
7002	.15
7003	.15
7004	.15
7005	.12
7006	.12
7007	.15
7008	.15
7009	.12
7010	.12
7011	.15
7012	.10
7013	.15
7014	.16

HAROLD FLAMMER INCORPORATED PUBLISHER NEW YORK

AO47-002

AO47-003

AO47-004

AO48-001

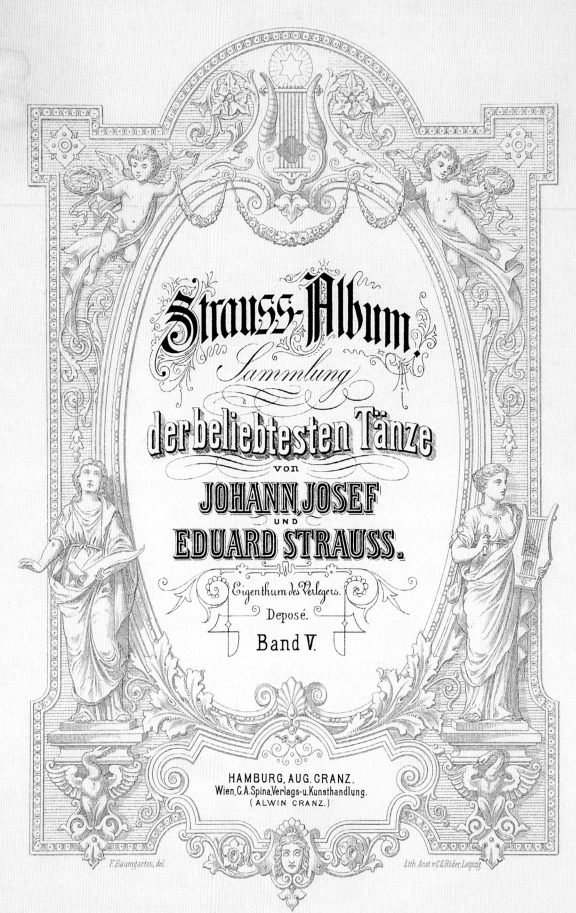

Strauss-Album.

Sammlung

der beliebtesten Tänze

von

JOHANN, JOSEF

UND

EDUARD STRAUSS.

Eigenthum des Verlegers.

Deposé.

Band V.

F. Baumgarten, del.

Lith. Anst. v. C.G. Röder, Leipzig.

HAMBURG, AUG. CRANZ.
Wien, C.A. Spina, Verlags-u. Kunsthandlung.
(ALWIN CRANZ.)

In die Edition Peters aufgenommen.

AO49-002

AO49-009

AO49-003

AO49-008

AO49-007

AO49-006

AO49-004

AO49-005

49 | AO49-001

AO50-002

AO50-003

AO50-004

AO50-005

AO50-006

IX. UN VOLEUR DANS

Vers deux heures du matin, J
réveilla.

Il avait dormi plus de[1] quatre het
était passée. Il ne p
5 penser. Beaucoup de
y en avait une qui cha
l'argenterie.

Les quatre couvert
gloire avait mis sur la
10 lui. Ils étaient bien s
Ils valaient au moins[2]
de ce qu'il avait gagné
placard, dans la chamb

Trois heures sonnèr
15 Jean Valjean rouvri
trouva assis sur le bor
pas un seul bruit dans
droit vers la fenêtre.
donnait sur le jardin.
20 n'était pas haut, on
facilement.[4]

Ce coup d'œil[5] jeté,
droite, et marchant trè
la porte de la chamb
25 Arrivé à cette porte,

[1] **plus de**, more than.
sound, strike (*of a bell*).
coup d'œil, glance, surve
entr'ouverte, half

Jean Valjean écouta. Pas de bruit ... Personne ne
remuait dans la maison.

Il poussa[1] la porte. Elle s'ouvrit un peu. Il at-
tendit un moment, puis poussa la porte une seconde
fois, avec plus de force. 5

e grande.[2] Mais,
aigu,[3] comme le cri

Jean Valjean comme
bruit, comme le cri 10

Dans un moment,
t s'écrierait, on al-
darmes viendraient,
la vie ... 15
pas de mouvement.

La porte restait
avait regarder dans

Il ne pensa plus
a dans la chambre de 20

quille ! Sans faire
lit. Il s'arrêta tout

CLOUD
nuage[4] couvrait le 25
an s'arrêta près du
comme une lumière
rallumée, parut tout
; s'ouvrit toute grande,
ng. [4] **nuage**, cloud.

AO51-001

AO52-002

AO52-003

AO52-006

AO52-004

AO52-005

AO52-001
52

Les Pauvres Gens

GEO. W. TERRY,
DEALER IN
BOOTS AND SHOES,
40 MAIN ST., HEMPSTEAD, L. I.

USE Ecker & Co.'s Dom Pedro Soap.

AO53-002

AO53-003   AO53-006

AO53-004

AO53-005

AO53-001

AO54-002

AO54-003

AO54-004

CENTURY EDITION

Standard Works.

Recreations

for the Pianoforte.

WalterBaker & Co.Ltd.

DORCHESTER, MASS.U.S.A. ESTABLISHED 1780.

FINE CHOCOLATES.

GRAPE.   FRUITS and THEIR BLOSSOMS   PEAR.

M. A. BUNNELL,
Fine + Millinery,
1 Wieting Block,   Syracuse, N.Y.

Liure de
Diuers Ornements
Dorfeurerie fait par
Jean Mussard Orfeure
1678
Auec priuilege

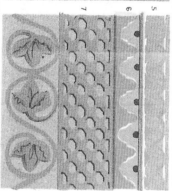

Century Music Publishing Company New York

AO55-002

AO55-003

AO55-007

AO55-004

AO55-006

AO55-005

55 — AO55-001

AO56-002

AO56-003

AO56-004

AO56-006

AO56-005

AO57-007

AO57-002

AO57-006

AO57-003

AO57-005

AO57-004

AO57-001